Tadpole Tadpole

D1542724

Edited by Linda Meyer

Copyright © 2016 by Cammie Ho

Text copyright © 2016 by Cammie Ho. All rights reserved, including the right of reproduction, in whole or in part, in any form.

Paperback ISBN: 978-1-943241-01-9
EPUB ISBN: 978-1-943241-06-4
Mobipocket ISBN: 978-1-943241-21-7
e-PDF ISBN: 978-1-943241-26-2

Library of Congress Control Number: 2015943299

Phonic Monic Books
www.phonicmonic.com

C&C Joint Printing Co. (Guangdong) Ltd.
Chunhu Industrial Eatate, Pinghu
Long Gang, Shenzhen, PRC 518111
www.candcprinting.com

First Edition – April 2016

Image Credits:
Cover pg. Mr. Suttipon Yakham /Shutterstock, Editor pg. FikMik/Shutterstock, Dedication pg. Fikmik/Shutterstock, Kerstin Klaassen/Shutterstock; 1, Dr. Morley Read/Shutterstock; 2, Eric Isselee/Shutterstock; 3, Suntipab/Shutterstock; 4, Zoonar RF/Shutterstock; 5, Kerstin Klaassen/Thinkstockphotos; 6, eve_eve01genesis/Thinkstockphotos; 7, eve_eve01genesis/Thinkstockphotos; 8, Dr. Morley Read/Shutterstock; 9, GlobalP/Shutterstock; 10, Dirk Ercken/Shutterstock; 11, worldswildlifewonders/Shutterstock; 12, Mat Hayward/Shutterstock; 13, Aleksey Stemmer//Shutterstock; 14, Dirk Ercken/Shutterstock; 15, Sascha Burkard/Shutterstock; 16, worldswildlifewonders/Shutterstock; 17, freebilly/Thinkstockphotos; 18, Dirk ErckenSmit/Shutterstock; 19, Cathy Keifer/Shutterstock; 20, Aleksandras Naryshkin/Thinkstockphotos; 21, freebilly/Shutterstock; 22, Dirk Ercken/Shutterstock; 23, Eduard Kyslynskyy/Shutterstock; 24, Dirk Ercken/Shutterstock; 25, Kletr/Shutterstock; 26, Marius Neacsa/Shutterstock; 27, Dr. Morley Read/Shutterstock; 28, Dirk Ercken/Shutterstock; 29, Maria Maarbes/Shutterstock; 30, FikMik/Shutterstock; 31, FikMik/Shutterstock; 33.

This book is dedicated to my family.
Thanks for all your support!

Tadpole, tadpole,

Eggs in a batch.

Tadpole, tadpole,

You can hatch.

Tadpole, tadpole,

Sons and daughters.

Tadpole, tadpole,

In the water.

Tadpole, tadpole,

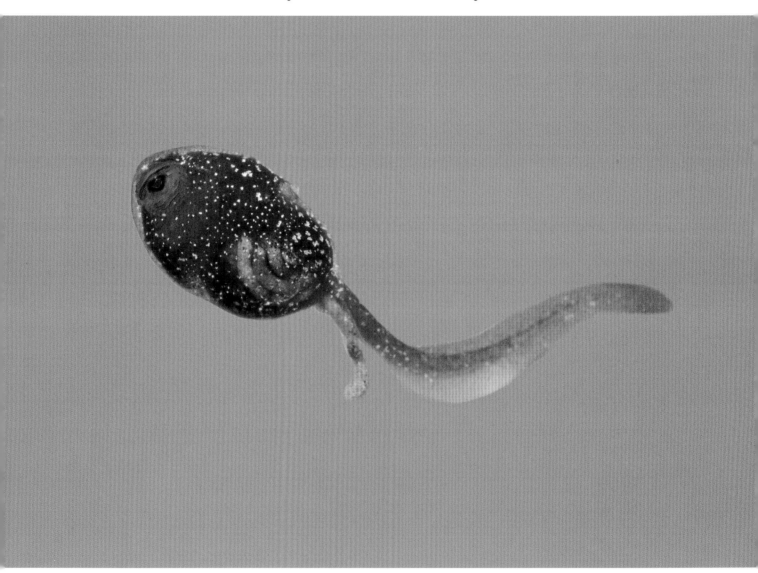

You've got a tail.

Tadpole, tadpole,

Your gills inhale.

Tadpole, tadpole,

You've got charm.

Tadpole, tadpole,

Grow legs and arms.

Tadpole, tadpole,

Don't you wail.

Tadpole, tadpole,

Lose your tail.

Tadpole, tadpole,

Look at you now!

You're a hopping frog!

Wow!

Hopping frog, hopping frog,

My, oh my!

Hopping frog, hopping frog,

Nice big eyes.

Hopping frog, hopping frog,

Quick and limber.

Hopping frog, hopping frog,

Nice four fingers.

Hopping frog, hopping frog,

Sticky feet.

Hopping frog, hopping frog,

You can leap.

Hopping frog, hopping frog,

Don't delay.

Hopping frog, hopping frog,

Catch your prey.

Hopping frog, hopping frog,

Make ribbit sounds.

Hopping frog, hopping frog,

Hop around.

Hopping frog, hopping frog,

Have a nice day.

Hopping frog, hopping frog,

Hop away.

Hopping frog, hopping frog,

Hop here and there.

Hopping frog, hopping frog,

Hop everywhere.

Hopping frog, hopping frog,

Lay eggs in a batch.

Springtime, springtime,

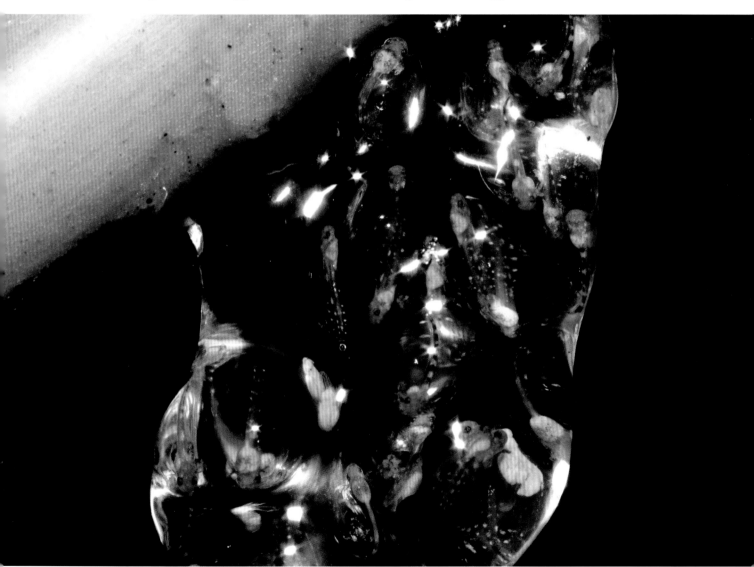

Eggs will hatch.

About the Author

Cammie Ho lives with her husband and two children in California, where she studied and obtained her Elementary School Teaching Credential and her Master's Degree in Teaching English as a Second Language.

Cammie loves reading books to her children, and is inspired by her favorite children's book authors, Dr. Seuss and Bill Martin Jr. She is developing an early learning program using music and chants to teach young children, believing that children learn well through a variety of fun channels. She writes lyrics and produces songs that teach reading and spelling in a program called, Phonic Monic.

www.phonicmonic.com